D0460693

Expressions of Faith

Expressions of Faith

Art by Greg Olsen

Baker Books

A Division of Baker Book House Co
Grand Rapids, Michigan 49516

© 1999 by Baker Book House

Art copyright by Greg Olsen

Published by Baker Books
a division of Baker Book House Company
P.O. Box 6287, Grand Rapids, MI 49516-6287

Printed in the United States of America

ISBN 0-8010-1186-8

For current information about all releases from Baker Book House, visit our web site:
http://www.bakerbooks.com

Interior design by Brian Brunsting

Contents

Introduction

This collection of classic poetry and contemporary art represents some of the finest and most renowned examples of inspired Christian artistry, past and present.

Each poet whose work is represented here remains a voice for all generations. Their message is still clear and important today, as certainly as in the past—God our Father is Lord over all.

So, too, the artist's visual representation of Christ, as nurturer, as Good Shepherd, as the giver and sustainer of life, shows us the timeless nature of the character of Jesus, even as it enables us to better contemplate and appreciate the foundations of our faith.

Jesus Shall Reign Where'er the Sun

Jesus shall reign where'er the sun
Does his successive journeys run;
His Kingdom stretch from shore to shore,
Till moons shall wax and wane no more.

People and realms of every tongue
Dwell on His love with sweetest song,
And infant voices shall proclaim
Their early blessings on His Name.

Let every creature rise and bring
Peculiar honors to our King,
Angels descend with songs again
And earth repeat the loud Amen!

Isaac Watts

O Jerusalem

"O Jerusalem, Jerusalem . . . how often would I have gathered thy children together, even as a hen gathereth her chickens under her wings." As the slanting rays of the sun reflect upon the rooftops of Old Jerusalem, Christ reflects upon his life's mission and upon those he came to serve and bless. His gaze takes in the glistening gold and marble of Herod's temple and the smoke of burnt offerings upon the altar. He was keenly aware that soon he would offer himself up as the true Passover lamb—"the Lamb of God." Here, upon the Mount of Olives, Jesus could see the day, like his mortal ministry, coming to a close. However, a new day always dawns and there is hope and comfort in his words, "Lo, I am with you always." Just as he looked down upon the traveling pilgrims entering Jerusalem, he watches still, ready to extend his protective wing to all who seek him.

Greg Olsen

First Day

Hail, sacred Light, which highly dost excel
And dost our sorrows and our fears dispel!
When first appearing, thou didst strike the sight
With darting beams, all glorious, fair, and bright,
And wondrous charming. Oh! how great and full
Of sparkling glory! Oh! how beautiful!
How sweet thy shine! How ravishing thy rays!
Proclaiming loud thy great Creator's praise
When marvelously He had now decreed
That day should night, and night should day succeed,
That this His works and wonders might display
And shadow forth His own eternal day,
Whilst that should temper the day's increasing drought,
Moisten the air, and make the earth to sprout.

He gave the Word, and day did straight appear,
Till day at length declined, and night drew near.
Night, which hovering with her sable wing,
Doth ease and rest to wearied mortals bring.
Thus nights and days, and days and nights do fly,
Returning in their course successively—
Each with its comforts, though of different kinds,
Both for our active and our drooping minds.
Since then both day and night such blessings bring,
By day and night let's bless our Lord and King,
The King of all the World, in whom we move
And live and are, the mighty God above.

Thomas Traherne

A Hymn to God the Father

Hear me, O God!
   A broken heart
   Is my best part:
Use still Thy Rod,
   That I may prove,
   Therein, Thy love.

If Thou hadst not
   Been stern to me,
   But left me free,
I had forgot
   Myself and Thee.

For sin's so sweet,
   As minds ill bent
   Rarely repent
Until they meet
   Their punishment.

Who more can crave
    Than Thou hast done:
    That gav'st a Son
To free a slave?
    First made of nought,
    Withal since bought.

Sin, Death, and Hell
    His glorious Name
    Quite overcame,
Yet I rebel
    And slight the same.

But I'll come in
    Before my loss
    Me farther toss,
As sure to win
    Under His Cross.

                    Ben Jonson

If I Could Trust Mine Own Self

If I could trust mine own self with your fate,
    Shall I not rather trust it in God's hand?
    Without Whose Will one lily doth not stand,
Nor sparrow fall at His appointed date;
    Who numbereth the innumerable sand,
Who weighs the wind and water with a weight,
To Whom the world is neither small nor great,
    Whose knowledge foreknew every plan we planned.
Searching my heart for all that touches you,
    I find there only love and love's goodwill
Helpless to help and impotent to do,
Of understanding dull, of sight most dim;
And therefore I commend you back to Him
    Whose love your love's capacity can fill.

Christina Rossetti

Forever and Ever

Surrounded by his enduring love, we are warm, safe, and secure. That reassuring calm comes not by a spoken word or by gazing with our eyes upon his strong arms. It comes from the embrace which our heart feels and through the tender senses of our spirit. All around us we have the physical wonders and beauties of nature that bear the signature of their Creator and remind us of his enduring love. Although his presence is unseen by our eyes, his unending love is felt in our hearts.

Greg Olsen

As Weary Pilgrim

As weary pilgrim, now at rest,
    Hugs with delight his silent nest,
His wasted limbs now lie full soft
    That mirey steps have trodden oft,
Blesses himself to think upon
    His dangers past and travails done.
The burning sun no more shall heat,
    Nor stormy rains on him shall beat.
The briars and thorns no more shall scratch,
    Nor hungry wolves at him shall catch.
His erring paths no more shall tread,
    Nor wild fruits eat instead of bread.
For waters cold he doth not long,
    For thirst no more shall parch his tongue.
No rugged stones his feet shall gall,
    Nor stumps nor rocks cause him to fall.
All cares and fears he bids farewell
    And means in safety now to dwell.
A pilgrim I, on earth perplexed
    With sins, with cares and sorrows vext,
By age and pains brought to decay,
    And my clay house mold'ring away.

Oh, how I long to be at rest
    And soar on high among the blest.
This body shall in silence sleep,
    Mine eyes no more shall ever weep,
No fainting fits shall me assail,
    Nor grinding pains my body frail;
With cares and fears ne'er cumbered be
    Nor losses know, nor sorrows see.
What though my flesh shall there consume,
    It is the bed Christ did perfume,
And when a few years shall be gone,
    This mortal shall be clothed upon.
A corrupt carcass down it lies,
    A glorious body it shall rise.
In weakness and dishonor sown,
    In power 'tis raised by Christ alone.
Then soul and body shall unite
    And of their Maker have the sight.
Such lasting joys shall there behold
    As ear ne'er heard nor tongue e'er told.
Lord, make me ready for that day;
    Then come, dear Bridegroom, come away.

                                    Anne Bradstreet

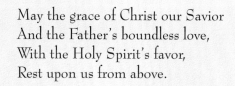

May the grace of Christ our Savior
And the Father's boundless love,
With the Holy Spirit's favor,
Rest upon us from above.

Thus may we abide in union
With each other and the Lord,
And possess, in sweet communion,
Joys which earth cannot afford.

John Newton

Blest be that sacred covenant love,
　　Uniting though we part;
We may be called far off to move,
　　We still are one in heart.

Joined in one Spirit to our Head,
　　Where He appoints, we go;
And while we in His footsteps tread,
　　Show forth His praise below.

O may we ever walk with Him
　　And nothing know beside:
Naught else desire, naught else esteem
　　But Jesus Crucified.

　　　　　　　　Charles Wesley

Rise heart; thy Lord is risen. Sing His praise
Without delays,
Who takes thee by the hand, that thou likewise
With Him mayst rise:
That as His death calcined thee to dust,
His life may make thee gold, and much more, just.

Awake, my lute, and struggle for thy part
With all thy art.
The cross taught all wood to resound His Name,
Who bore the same.
His stretchèd sinews taught all strings what key
Is best to celebrate this most high day.

Consort both heart and lute, and twist a song
Pleasant and long:
Or, since all music is but three parts vied
And multiplied,
O let Thy blessed Spirit bear a part,
And make up our defects with His sweet art.

George Herbert

The Good Shepherd

The age-old symbol of the Good Shepherd has brought peace and com-
fort to the hearts of many throughout the years. The strong and watch-
ful keeper of the flock, who knows his sheep and is known by them,
guides the sheep to green pastures and to still waters where they can
graze and safely drink. He gathers them before the approaching storm
and searches for those that may be lost. He places himself between dan-
ger and the flock he tends. His sheep recognize his voice, and his call is
a call to peace, safety, and contentment.

Greg Olsen

"In No Strange Land"

O world invisible, we view thee,
O world intangible, we touch thee,
O world unknowable, we know thee,
Inapprehensible, we clutch thee!

Does the fish soar to find the ocean,
The eagle plunge to find the air—
That we ask of the stars in motion
If they have rumor of thee there?

Not where the wheeling systems darken
And our benumbed conceiving soars!
The drift of pinions, would we hearken,
Beats at our own clay-shuttered doors.

The angels keep their ancient places;
Turn but a stone, and start a wing!
'Tis ye, 'tis your estranged faces,
That miss the many-splendored thing.

But, when so sad thou canst not sadder,
Cry—and upon thy so sore loss
Shall shine the traffic of Jacob's ladder
Pitched betwixt Heaven and Charing Cross.

Yea, in the night, my Soul, my daughter,
Cry, clinging Heaven by the hems;
And lo, Christ walking on the water
Not of Gennesareth, but Thames!

Francis Thompson

Psalm 136

Let us with a gladsome mind
Praise the Lord for He is kind:
For His mercies aye endure,
Ever faithful, ever sure.

Let us blaze His name abroad,
For of gods He is the God:
For His mercies aye endure,
Ever faithful, ever sure.

He, with all-commanding might,
Filled the new-made world with light:
For His mercies aye endure,
Ever faithful, ever sure.

He the golden-tressèd sun
Caused all day his course to run:
For His mercies aye endure,
Ever faithful, ever sure.

And the moon to shine by night,
'Mid her spangled sisters bright:
For His mercies aye endure,
Ever faithful, ever sure.

All things living He doth feed;
His full hand supplies their need:
For His mercies aye endure,
Ever faithful, ever sure.

Let us therefore warble forth
His high majesty and worth:
For His mercies aye endure,
Ever faithful, ever sure.

John Milton

Let All the World in Every Corner Sing

Let all the world in every corner sing, My God and King!
The heavens are not too high,
His praise may thither fly;
The earth is not too low,
His praises there may grow.
Let all the world in every corner sing, My God and King!

Let all the world in every corner sing, My God and King!
The Church with psalms must shout,
No door can keep them out;
But, above all, the heart
Must bear the longest part.
Let all the world in every corner sing, My God and King!

George Herbert

A Light to the Gentiles

The promise of a Savior was fulfilled by our heavenly Father in Christ, who is the Light of the World.

Greg Olsen

Glorious Things of Thee Are Spoken

Glorious things of thee are spoken,
    Zion, city of our God;
He whose Word cannot be broken
    Formed thee for His own abode.
On the Rock of Ages founded,
    What can shake thy sure repose?
With salvation's walls surrounded
    Thou may'st smile at all thy foes.

See, the streams of living waters,
    Springing from eternal love,
Well supply thy sons and daughters
    And all fear of want remove.
Who can faint while such a river
    Ever flows their thirst t'assuage?
Grace which like the Lord, the Giver,
    Never fails from age to age.

Savior, if of Zion's city
    I, through grace, a member am,
Let the world deride or pity,
    I will glory in Thy Name.
Fading is the worldling's pleasure,
    All his boasted pomp and show;
Solid joys and lasting treasure
    None but Zion's children know.

                John Newton

Light Shining out of Darkness

God moves in a mysterious way
   His wonders to perform;
He plants His footsteps in the sea
   And rides upon the storm.

Deep in unfathomable mines
   Of never-failing skill
He treasures up His bright designs,
   And works His sovereign will.

Ye fearful saints, fresh courage take
   The clouds ye so much dread
Are big with mercy and shall break
   In blessings on your head.

Judge not the Lord by feeble sense,
   But trust Him for His grace;
Behind a frowning providence,
   He hides a smiling face.

His purposes will ripen fast,
   Unfolding every hour;
The bud may have a bitter taste,
   But sweet will be the flower.

Blind unbelief is sure to err
   And scan His work in vain;
God is His own Interpreter,
   And He will make it plain.

William Cowper

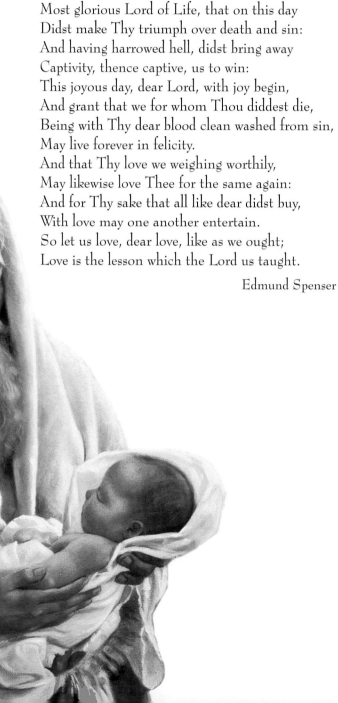

Most glorious Lord of Life, that on this day
Didst make Thy triumph over death and sin:
And having harrowed hell, didst bring away
Captivity, thence captive, us to win:
This joyous day, dear Lord, with joy begin,
And grant that we for whom Thou diddest die,
Being with Thy dear blood clean washed from sin,
May live forever in felicity.
And that Thy love we weighing worthily,
May likewise love Thee for the same again:
And for Thy sake that all like dear didst buy,
With love may one another entertain.
So let us love, dear love, like as we ought;
Love is the lesson which the Lord us taught.

Edmund Spenser

Joy to the World

Joy to the world! the Lord is come;
Let earth receive her King.
Let every heart prepare Him room
And heaven and nature sing.

Joy to the earth! the Savior reigns;
Let men their songs employ,
While fields and floods, rocks, hills, and plains
Repeat the sounding joy.

No more let sins and sorrows grow,
Nor thorns infest the ground;
He comes to make His blessings flow
Far as the curse is found.

He rules the world with truth and grace
And makes the nations prove
The glories of His righteousness
And wonders of His love.

Isaac Watts

We doubt the Word that tells us: Ask,
And ye shall have your prayer:
We turn our thoughts as to a task,
With will constrained and rare.

And yet we have; these scanty prayers
Yield gold without alloy:
O God, but he that trusts and dares
Must have a boundless joy!

George MacDonald

Precious in His Sight

Under his watchful eye, a tiny sprout grows to a lovely, fragrant flower, the drab cocoon brings forth the beautiful butterfly, and the Babe in the manger becomes the Prince of Peace! These miracles bring wonderment and awe to our hearts, warming our souls like rays of sun on a spring morning, reminding us of an eternal truth—that all things are precious in his sight.

Greg Olsen

Paradise

I bless Thee, Lord, because I grow
Among Thy trees, which in a row
To Thee both fruit and order owe.

What open force or hidden charm
Can blast my fruit or bring me harm
While the enclosure is Thine arm?

Enclose me still for fear I start.
Be to me rather sharp and tart
Than let me want Thy hand and art.

When Thou dost greater judgments spare
And with Thy knife but prune and pare,
Even fruitful trees more fruitful are.

Such sharpness shows the sweetest friend,
Such cuttings rather heal than rend,
And such beginnings touch their end.

George Herbert

Meditation I

What love is this of Thine that cannot be
    In Thine infinity, O Lord, confined,
Unless it in Thy very Person see
    Infinity and finity conjoined?
    What hath Thy Godhead, as not satisfied,
    Married our manhood, making it its bride?

Oh, matchless Love! filling heaven to the brim!
    O'er-running it—all running o'er beside
This world! Nay, overflowing hell, wherein
    For Thine elect there rose a mighty tide!
    That there our veins might through Thy Person bleed
    To quench those flames that else would on us feed.

Oh! that Thy love might overflow my heart!
    To fire the same with love, for love I would.
But oh! my straitened breast! my lifeless spark!
    My fireless flame! What chilly love and cold?
    In measure small! In manner chilly! See.
    Lord, blow the coal: Thy love enflame in me.

Edward Taylor

When I consider how my light is spent
   Ere half my days in this dark world and wide,
   And that one talent which is death to hide
   Lodged with me useless, though my soul more bent
To serve therewith my Maker, and present
   My true account, lest he returning chide;
   "Doth God exact day-labor, light denied?"
   I fondly ask; but Patience to prevent
That murmur, soon replies, "God doth not need
   Either man's work or his own gifts; who best
   Bear his mild yoke, they serve him best. His state
Is kingly. Thousands at his bidding speed
   And post o'er land and ocean without rest;
   They also serve who only stand and wait."

John Milton

The Dwelling Place

John 1:38–39

What happy, secret fountain,
   Fair shade, or mountain,
Whose undiscovered virgin glory
Boasts it this day, though not in story,
Was then Thy dwelling? Did some cloud,
Fixed to a tent, descend and shroud
My distressed Lord? Or did a star
Beckoned by Thee, though high and far,
In sparkling smiles haste gladly down
To lodge Light, and increase her own?
My dear, dear God! I do not know
What lodged Thee then, nor where, nor how;
But I am sure, Thou dost now come
Oft to a narrow, homely room,
Where Thou too hast but the least part;
My God, I mean my sinful heart.

Henry Vaughan

My Spirit Longs for Thee

My spirit longs for Thee
Within my troubled breast,
Though I unworthy be
Of so divine a Guest.
Of so divine a Guest
Unworthy though I be,
Yet has my heart no rest
Unless it come from Thee.

Unless it come from Thee,
In vain I look around;
In all that I can see
No rest is to be found.
No rest is to be found
But in Thy blessed love:
O let my wish be crowned
And send it from above!

John Byrom

The Light of the World

Just as a light set upon a hill serves as a beacon to weary travelers, so Jesus Christ stands as a shining example to all the world, showing us a better way to peace and happiness. His light illuminates the path of life, leading us along the straight and narrow way, exposing obstacles that may cause us to stumble, or forks in the road that might lead us astray. Those who press on, with their gaze fixed upon the light of Christ, have their own lights kindled within. Rather than merely casting a shadow, they serve as helpful luminaries to the rest of humanity on life's journey.

Greg Olsen

Rondel

I do not know Thy final will;
　　It is too good for me to know:
　　Thou willest that I mercy show,
That I take heed and do no ill,
That I the needy warm and fill,
　　Nor stones at any sinner throw;
But I know not Thy final will—
　　It is too good for me to know.

I know Thy love unspeakable—
　　For love's sake able to send woe!
　　To find Thine own Thou lost didst go,
And wouldst for men Thy blood yet spill!—
How should I know Thy final will,
　　Godwise too good for me to know!

　　　　　　　　George MacDonald

Meeting with Time, "Slack thing," said I,
"Thy scythe is dull; whet it for shame."
"No marvel, sir," he did reply,
"If it at length deserve some blame;
   But where one man would have me grind it,
   Twenty for one too sharp do find it."

"Perhaps some such of old did pass,
Who above all things loved this life,
To whom thy scythe a hatchet was,
Which now is but a pruning knife.
   Christ's coming hath made man thy debtor,
   Since by thy cutting he grows better."

George Herbert

Walking with God

Oh, for a closer walk with God,
   A calm and heavenly frame,
A light to shine upon the road
   That leads me to the Lamb!

Where is the blessedness I knew
   When first I saw the Lord?
Where is the soul-refreshing view
   Of Jesus, and His Word?

What peaceful hours I once enjoyed!
   How sweet their memory still!
But they have left an aching void
   The world can never fill.

Return, O holy Dove, return,
    Sweet messenger of rest;
I hate the sins that made thee mourn
    And drove thee from my breast.

The dearest idol I have known,
    Whate'er that idol be;
Help me to tear it from Thy throne
    And worship only Thee.

So shall my walk be close with God,
    Calm and serene my frame;
So purer light shall mark the road
    That leads me to the Lamb.

                    William Cowper

Nothing is so beautiful as spring—
    When weeds, in wheels, shoot long and lovely and lush;
    Thrush's eggs look little low heavens, and thrush
Through the echoing timber does so rinse and wring
The ear, it strikes like lightnings to hear him sing;
    The glassy peartree leaves and blooms, they brush
    The descending blue; that blue is all in a rush
With richness; the racing lambs too have fair their fling.

What is all this juice and all this joy?
    A strain of the earth's sweet being in the beginning
In Eden garden. —Have, get, before it cloy,
    Before it cloud, Christ, Lord, and sour with sinning,
Innocent mind and Mayday in girl and boy,
    Most, O maid's Child, thy choice and worthy the winning.

Gerard Manley Hopkins

Sacred Grove

The shady cathedral of the woods has long offered a retreat to the soul seeking communion with nature and her Creator. The trees rise like mighty spires, lifting our gaze and our thoughts heavenward. Layers of leaves are illuminated like stained glass windows as the morning sun filters through them. The delicate notes of songbirds float like a hymn upon the still air. Rays of light stream down from the windows of heaven, warming the forest floor below. They rest upon one's being and take away the chill of darker hours. It is in quiet places and in simple ways that heaven's veil is parted for those who knock upon its door.

Greg Olsen

As Spring the Winter

May 13, 1657

As spring the winter doth succeed
And leaves the naked trees do dress,
The earth all black is clothed in green.
At sunshine each their joy express.

My sun's returned with healing wings,
My soul and body doth rejoice,
My heart exults and praises sings
To Him that heard my wailing voice.

My winter's past, my storms are gone,
And former clouds seem now all fled,
But if they must eclipse again,
I'll run where I was succoréd.

I have a shelter from the storm,
A shadow from the fainting heat,
I have access unto His throne,
Who is a God so wondrous great.

O hath Thou made my pilgrimage
Thus pleasant, fair, and good,
Blessed me in youth and elder age,
My Baca made a springing flood.

O studious am what I shall do
To show my duty with delight;
All I can give is but Thine own
And at the most a simple mite.

Anne Bradstreet

God's Grandeur

The world is charged with the grandeur of God.
  It will flame out, like shining from shook foil;
  It gathers to a greatness, like the ooze of oil
Crushed. Why do men then now not reck His rod?
Generations have trod, have trod, have trod;
  And all is seared with trade; bleared, smeared with toil;
  And wears man's smudge and shares man's smell: the soil
Is bare now, nor can foot feel, being shod.

And for all this, nature is never spent;
  There lives the dearest freshness deep down things;
And though the last lights off the black West went
  Oh, morning, at the brown brink eastward, springs—
Because the Holy Ghost over the bent
  World broods with warm breast and with ah! bright wings.

Gerard Manley Hopkins

My Soul Thirsts for God

I thirst, but not as once I did,
The vain delights of earth to share;
Thy wounds, Emmanuel, all forbid
That I should seek my pleasures there.

It was the sight of Thy dear Cross
First weaned my soul from earthly things
And taught me to esteem as dross
The mirth of fools, and pomp of kings.

I want that grace that springs from Thee,
That quickens all things where it flows,
And makes a wretched thorn like me
Bloom as the myrtle or the rose.

Dear Fountain of delights unknown!
No longer sink below the brim,
But overflow and pour me down
A living and life-giving stream!

For sure, of all the plants that share
The notice of Thy Father's eye,
None proves less grateful to His care
Or yields him meaner fruit than I.

William Cowper

Peace

My soul, there is a country
　Far beyond the stars,
Where stands a winged sentry
　All skillful in the wars;
There above noise and danger
　Sweet peace sits crowned with smiles,
And One born in a manger
　Commands the beauteous files;
He is thy gracious Friend,
　And (O my soul, awake!)
Did in pure love descend
　To die here for thy sake;

If thou canst get but thither,
　There grows the flower of peace,
The Rose that cannot wither,
　Thy Fortress and thy Ease.
Leave then thy foolish ranges;
　For none can thee secure,
But One Who never changes,
　Thy God, thy Life, thy Cure.

Henry Vaughan

Be Not Afraid

Like children who have lost their way
Alone and comfortless we wander.
Stumbling through woods that grow deep and ever darker,
With no direction, we cry for help
And hear our pleas echo through the canyons.
Is there anyone who can hear us?
Then, like a rushing wind, a voice whispers to our heart.
And through tear-filled eyes, we see an outstretched hand,
There to lead us home.
Though swirling streams may block our way
And slippery stones betray our feet,
He leads us on. He knows the way, his feet are sure,
And in him we find safe passage.

Greg Olsen

Seek the Lord, and in His ways persever.
   O faint not, but as eagles fly;
   For His steep hill is high;
Then striving gain the top, and triumph ever.

When with glory there thy brows are crowned,
   New joys so shall abound in thee,
   Such sights thy soul shall see,
That worldly thoughts shall by their beams be drowned.

Farewell, World, thou mass of mere confusion,
   False light, with many shadows dimmed,
   Old Witch, with new foils trimmed,
Thou deadly sleep of soul, and charmed illusion.

I the King will seek, of kings adored;
   Spring of light, tree of grace and bliss,
   Whose fruit so sovereign is
That all who taste it are from death restored.

Thomas Campion

Who Would True Valor See

Who would true valor see,
   Let him come hither;
One here will constant be,
   Come wind, come weather;
There's no discouragement
Shall make him once relent
His first avowed intent
    To be a pilgrim.

Whoso beset him round
   With dismal stories,
Do but themselves confound—
   His strength the more is.
No lion can him fright;
He'll with a giant fight,
But he will have a right
    To be a pilgrim.

Hobgoblin nor foul fiend
   Can daunt his spirit;
He knows he at the end
   Shall life inherit.
Then fancies fly away,
He'll fear not what men say;
He'll labor night and day
    To be a pilgrim.

John Bunyan

Who Shall Deliver Me?

God strengthen me to bear myself;
That heaviest weight of all to bear,
Inalienable weight of care.

All others are outside myself;
I lock my door and bar them out,
The turmoil, tedium, gad-about.

I lock my door upon myself,
And bar them out; but who shall wall
Self from myself, most loathed of all?

If I could once lay down myself,
And start self-purged upon the race
That all must run! Earth runs apace.

If I could set aside myself,
And start with lightened heart upon
The road by all men overgone!

God harden me against myself,
This coward with pathetic voice
Who craves for ease, and rest, and joys:

Myself, arch-traitor to myself;
My hollowest friend, my deadliest foe,
My clog whatever road I go.

Yet One there is can curb myself,
Can roll the strangling load from me,
Break off the yoke and set me free.

Christina Rossetti

Good Friday

Am I a stone, and not a sheep
  That I can stand, O Christ, beneath Thy Cross,
  To number drop by drop Thy Blood's slow loss,
And yet not weep?

Not so those women loved
  Who with exceeding grief lamented Thee;
  Not so fallen Peter weeping bitterly;
Not so the thief was moved;

Not so the Sun and Moon
  Which hid their faces in a starless sky,
A horror of great darkness at broad noon—
  I, only I.

Yet give not o'er,
  But seek Thy sheep, true Shepherd of the flock;
Greater than Moses, turn and look once more
  And smite a rock.

Christina Rossetti

The Sower

One virtue of the sower is his service to others. His labor is performed without any sign of growth or hint of the fruit to come. Yet he plants with faith, believing in the fertile soil, the nourishing rains, and the warming sun. With time the seeds will sprout and bring forth after their own kind in abundance. The sower is blessed in knowing that he has helped provide a bounty that others can enjoy.

Learning

Come, come with emulative strife,
To learn the Way, the Truth, and Life,
   Which Jesus is in One;
In all sound doctrines He proceeds
From Alpha to Omega leads,
   E'en Spirit, Sire, and Son.

Sure of the exceeding great reward,
Midst all your learning, learn the Lord—
   This was thy doctrine, Paul;
And this thy lecture should persuade,
Though thou hadst more of human aid
   Than thy blest brethren all.

Humanity's a charming thing,
And every science of the ring;
   Good is the classic lore.
For these are helps along the road
That leads to Zion's blest abode
   And Heavenly Muse's store.

But greater still in each respect,
He that communicates direct,
   The Tutor of the soul,
Who without pain, degrees, or parts,
While He illuminates our hearts,
   Can teach at once the whole.

                    Christopher Smart

Old-Testament Gospel

Israel in ancient days,
Not only had a view
Of Sinai in a blaze,
But learned the Gospel too;
The types and figures were a glass
In which they saw the Savior's face.

The paschal sacrifice
And blood-besprinkled door
Seen with enlightened eyes
And once applied with power
Would teach the need of other blood
To reconcile an angry God.

The Lamb, the Dove, set forth
His perfect innocence,
Whose blood, of matchless worth,
Should be the soul's defence;
For He who can for sin atone
Must have no failings of His own.

The scape-goat on his head
The people's trespass bore,
And to the desert led,
Was to be seen no more.
In him, our Surety seemed to say,
"Behold, I bear your sins away."

Dipped in his fellow's blood,
The living bird went free;
The type, well understood,
Expressed the sinner's plea,
Described a guilty soul enlarged
And by a Savior's death discharged.

Jesus, I love to trace
Throughout the sacred page
The footsteps of Thy grace,
The same in every age!
Oh grant that I may faithful be
To clearer light vouchsafed to me!

William Cowper

Perhaps no other being in history has been the subject of more artwork than Christ. Artistic masters throughout the ages have been drawn to the challenge of portraying themes of inspiration and significance. The life of Christ is an enduring model of humility, compassion, and love.

This painting is a visual reminder of one of his most comforting messages regarding the worth of each individual soul. "Are not five sparrows sold for two farthings, and not one of them is forgotten before God? But even the very hairs of your head are all numbered. Fear not therefore: ye are of more value than many sparrows" (Luke 12:6–7).

As I look at the intricate design of these little sparrows, experience tells me that where there is a design, there is a designer! It is a comforting thought to consider that somewhere there is a Creator who is aware of and has love for even the least of his creations. There is incredible intimacy in the vastness of this thought.

Greg Olsen

Gratefulness

Thou that hast given so much to me,
Give one thing more, a grateful heart.
See how Thy beggar works on Thee
    By art.

He makes Thy gifts occasion more,
And says, If he in this be crossed,
All Thou hast given him heretofore
    Is lost.

But Thou didst reckon, when at first
Thy Word our hearts and hands did crave,
What it would come to at the worst
    To save.

George Herbert

Occasional Meditations

By night when others soundly slept,
And had at once both ease and rest,
My waking eyes were open kept
And so to lie I found it best.

I sought Him whom my soul did love,
With tears I sought Him earnestly;
He bowed His ear down from above,
In vain I did not seek or cry.

My hungry soul He filled with good,
He in His bottle put my tears;
My smarting wounds washed in His blood,
And banished thence my doubts and fears.

What to my Savior shall I give,
Who freely hath done this for me?
I'll serve Him here whilst I shall live
And love Him to eternity.

Anne Bradstreet

Beauty

Christ, keep me from the self-survey
    Of beauties all Thine own;
If there is beauty, let me pray,
    And praise the Lord alone.

Pray—that I may the fiend withstand,
    Where'er his serpents be;
Praise—that the Lord's almighty hand
    Is manifest in me.

It is not so—my features are
    Much meaner than the rest;
A glow-worm cannot be a star,
    And I am plain at best.

Then come, my Love, Thy grace impart,
    Great Savior of mankind;
O come and purify my heart
    And beautify my mind.

Then will I Thy carnations nurse
    And cherish every rose,
And empty to the poor my Purse
    Till grace to glory grows.

                    Christopher Smart

From All That Dwell below the Skies

From all that dwell below the skies
Let the Creator's praise arise;
Let the Redeemer's Name be sung
Through every land by every tongue.

Eternal are Thy mercies, Lord;
Eternal truth attends Thy Word:
Thy praise shall sound from shore to shore,
Till suns shall rise and set no more.

In every land begin the song;
To every land the strains belong:
In cheerful sounds all voices raise
And fill the world with loudest praise.

Isaac Watts

The shepherd and his flock have been ever present symbols of the Lord and the people of his pasture. The ancient role of a shepherd was much more than an assignment to herd sheep. The shepherd loved his sheep, he knew them, named them, provided for and protected them. In return, the sheep responded to their shepherd and recognized his voice. His call alone could bring them back from their wanderings in unfamiliar paths. If lambs were lost, he sought them out and brought them back to the fold.

Those who hear the Master's call and then seek to follow in his path will find him and there enjoy contentment and safety at his feet.

Greg Olsen

None Other Lamb

None other Lamb, none other Name,
   None other Hope in heaven or earth or sea,
None other Hiding-place from guilt and shame,
   None besides Thee.

My faith burns low, my hope burns low—
   Only my heart's desire cries out in me,
By the deep thunder of its want and woe,
   Cries out to Thee.

Lord, Thou art Life though I be dead,
   Love's Fire Thou art, however cold I be:
Nor heaven have I, nor place to lay my head,
   Nor home, but Thee.

Christina Rossetti

Good-Nature to Animals

The man of mercy (says the Seer)
   Shows mercy to his beast;
Learn not of churls to be severe,
   But house and feed at least.

Shall I melodious prisoners take
   From out the linnet's nest,
And not keep busy care awake
   To cherish every guest?

What, shall I whip in cruel wrath
   The steed that bears me safe;
Or 'gainst the dog, who plights his troth,
   For faithful service chafe?

In the deep waters throw thy bread,
   Which thou shalt find again,
With God's good interest on thy head,
   And pleasure for thy pain.

Let thine industrious silk-worms reap
   Their wages to the full,
Nor let neglected dormice sleep
   To death within thy wool.

Know when the frosty weather comes,
   'Tis charity to deal
To wren and redbreast all thy crumbs,
   The remnant of thy meal.

Though these some spirits think but light
   And deem indifferent things,
Yet they are serious in the sight
   Of Christ, the King of Kings.

Christopher Smart

71

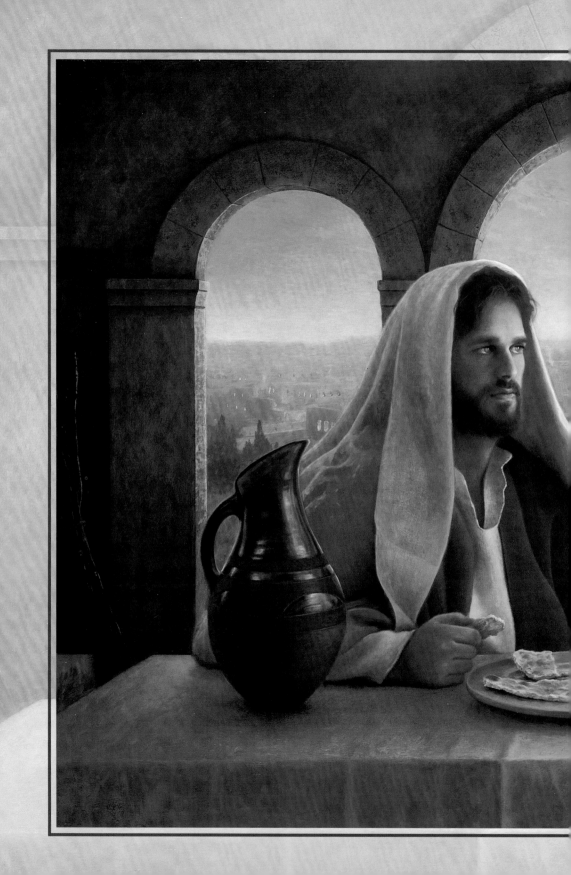

How Sweet the Name

How sweet the Name of Jesus sounds
In a believer's ear!
It soothes his sorrows, heals his wounds,
And drives away his fear.

It makes the wounded spirit whole
And calms the troubled breast;
'Tis manna to the hungry soul,
And to the weary rest. . . .

Weak is the effort of my heart
And cold my warmest thought;
But when I see Thee as Thou art,
I'll praise Thee as I ought.

Till then I would Thy love proclaim
With every fleeting breath;
And may the music of Thy Name
Refresh my soul in death.

John Newton

In Remembrance of Me

This Last Supper marks the beginning of the end. Judas has silently departed and is on his way to complete his treacherous bargain. The time has come for Christ to "suffer all things." Though understandably apprehensive, and wishing, even praying, that this cup might pass from him, nevertheless he submitted his will to that of his Father. He went on to drink the bitter cup and drain the very dregs—because he loves us! In return he asks only that we remember him, and in doing so, we are inspired to be more like him.

Greg Olsen

The Agony in the Garden

He knelt, the Savior knelt and prayed,
　　When but His Father's eye
Looked through the lonely garden's shade
　　On that dread agony;
The Lord All above, beneath,
Was bowed with sorrow unto death.

The sun set in a fearful hour,
　　The stars might well grow dim,
When this mortality had power
　　So to o'ershadow Him!
That He who gave man's breath, might know
The very depths of human woe.

He proved them all!—the doubt, the strife,
　　The faint perplexing dread,
The mists that hang o'er parting life,
　　All gathered round His head;
And the Deliverer knelt to pray—
Yet passed it not, that cup, away!

It passed not—though the stormy wave
　　Had sunk beneath His tread;
It passed not—though to Him the grave
　　Had yielded up its dead.
But there was sent Him from on high
A gift of strength for man to die.

And was the sinless thus beset
　　With anguish and dismay?
How may *we* meet our conflict yet
　　In the dark narrow way?
Through Him—through Him,
　　　　that path who trod—
Save, or we perish, Son of God!

Felicia Hemans

I saw Eternity the other night,
Like a great ring of pure and endless light,
    All calm as it was bright;
And round beneath it, time in hours, days, years,
    Driven by the spheres
Like a vast shadow moved, in which the world
    And all her train were hurled.
The doting lover in his quaintest strain
    Did there complain;
Near him, his lute, his fancy, and his flights,
    Wit's sour delights,
With gloves and knots, the silly snares of pleasure,
    Yet his dear treasure,
All scattered lay, while he his eyes did pour
    Upon a flower.

The darksome statesman, hung with weights of woe,
Like a thick midnight fog, moved there so slow,
    He did not stay nor go;
Condemning thoughts—like sad eclipses—scowl
    Upon his soul,
And clouds of crying witnesses without
    Pursued him with one shout.
Yet digged the mole, and lest his ways be found,
    Worked underground,
Where he did clutch his prey; but One did see
    That policy.
Churches and altars fed him; perjuries
    Were gnats and flies;
It rained about him blood and tears, but he
    Drank them as free.

The fearful miser on a heap of rust
Sat pining all his life there, did scarce trust
   His own hands with the dust,
Yet would not place one piece above, but lives
   In fear of thieves.
Thousands there were frantic as himself
   And hugged each one his pelf;
The downright epicure placed heaven in sense
   And scorned pretence;
While others, slipped into a wide excess,
   Said little less;
The weaker sort, slight, trivial wares enslave,
   Who think them brave;
And poor, despised Truth sat counting by
   Their victory.

Yet some, who all this while did weep and sing,
And sing and weep, soared up into the ring;
   But most would use no wing.
Oh, fools, said I, thus to prefer dark night
   Before true light!
To live in grots and caves and hate the day
   Because it shows the way;
The way which from this dead and dark abode
   Leads up to God—
A way where you might tread the sun, and be
   More bright than he!
But as I did their madness so discuss,
   One whispered thus,
"This ring the Bridegroom did for none provide,
   But for His bride."

                  Henry Vaughan

Index of Poems

Index of Poets